MW00916313

BENJAMIN FRANKLIN

BOOK FOR CURIOUS KIDS

Discover the Remarkable Life
and Adventures of America's
Ingenious Founding Father

MARK LYLANI

Copyright © 2024 MARK LYLANI

MARK LYLANI

TABLE OF CONTENTS

INTRODUCTION

Have you ever wondered what it would be like to have lived in a world without electricity? Or how someone could achieve so much in one lifetime—changing the course of history with their ideas and inventions? Imagine if you could sit down with Benjamin Franklin, one of America's most fascinating figures from history, and ask him about his adventures, experiments, and discoveries.

In this book, we embark on a journey through the life of Benjamin Franklin—a man of many talents and boundless curiosity. Join us as we uncover the remarkable story of a printer's apprentice turned scientist, inventor, diplomat, and Founding Father.

How did he transform a fascination with the mysteries of nature into groundbreaking experiments? What led him to challenge the status quo and advocate for independence?

As we flip through the pages of Franklin's life, we'll explore the intriguing questions that sparked his imagination and drove his quest for knowledge. From his humble beginnings in Boston to his pioneering experiments with electricity, from his role in shaping early American society to his adventures across Europe, Benjamin Franklin's life is a captivating tale of innovation, resilience, and passion.

Whether you're intrigued by lightning and storms, curious about how mail systems were established, or eager to learn about Franklin's diplomatic triumphs, this book is your guide. Join us as we delve into the world of Benjamin Franklin—the ultimate curious mind—and discover how his legacy continues to inspire and educate today.

Get ready to unravel the mysteries, explore the inventions, and meet the man who forever changed the way we think about science, society, and the pursuit of knowledge. Benjamin Franklin's story is not just history; it's an invitation to think, question, and explore—a journey tailor-made for curious kids like you.

So, are you ready to embark on this adventure? Let's turn the page and discover Benjamin Franklin's extraordinary life together.

From Ecton to Boston

Long ago, in the quiet village of Ecton, England, there lived a man named Josiah Franklin. Josiah was no ordinary villager—he was a skilled candlemaker known for crafting fine candles that brought light to the darkness. Born on December 23, 1657, Josiah learned his trade from his father, a hardworking blacksmith named Thomas Franklin.

Josiah's life took a turn when he married Anne Child. Together, they sailed across the ocean to the bustling city of Boston in 1683. They had three children before Anne passed away, leaving Josiah to care for their family alone.

Undeterred by hardship, Josiah found love again with Abiah Folger, a remarkable woman from Massachusetts. Abiah hailed from a family of pioneers—her father, Peter Folger, stood up for the rights of ordinary people against the powerful.

In 1689, Josiah and Abiah married, and their home soon echoed with the laughter of a large family. Together, they had ten more children, among them Benjamin Franklin, their eighth child, and Josiah's last son.

Benjamin grew up surrounded by the smell of melting wax and the warmth of a bustling household. His parents encouraged his curiosity and thirst for knowledge. Little did they know that their son Benjamin would become one of America's greatest inventors, thinkers, and leaders.

Ink and Independence

In the bustling streets of Boston, where the air was thick with the promise of new beginnings, a curious and spirited boy named Benjamin Franklin was born on January 17, 1706. His family lived along Milk Street, right in the heart of the bustling city in the Province of Massachusetts Bay. Benjamin's journey into the world began with wide eyes and a heart full of adventure.

Growing up near the Charles River, Benjamin was a natural leader among his friends. He loved to organize games and lead expeditions, always seeking out new discoveries.

Benjamin's father dreamed of his son becoming a clergyman, but money was tight, and Benjamin's formal schooling lasted only two years at the Boston Latin School. Yet, Benjamin's thirst for knowledge was unquenchable. He turned to books, reading everything he could get his hands on, exploring worlds beyond the classroom.

At the age of ten, Benjamin started helping his father with work. But when he turned twelve, destiny nudged him in a different direction. His older brother James, a printer, took him on as an apprentice.

Under James's guidance, Benjamin dove headfirst into the world of printing. By the time he was fifteen, James had started The New-England Courant, Boston's third newspaper. This newspaper would become a defining force in young Benjamin's life, shaping his ideas about freedom of speech and the power of words.

When Benjamin was denied the chance to write for the paper, he came up with a clever solution. He created a character named "Silence Dogood," a witty widow who wrote letters that captivated readers. Nobody knew that Silence Dogood was actually Benjamin Franklin!

His daring spirit came to light when his brother's newspaper faced trouble. In 1722, James was jailed for printing things that criticized the governor. Seizing the opportunity, Benjamin took over the paper and used Silence Dogood's voice to champion the importance of free speech and independent thinking.

Benjamin's bold stand against censorship set him on a path of independence. He left his apprenticeship without his brother's approval. He embarked on a journey that would make him not just a printer but a pioneer of new ideas, a fighter for liberty, and a champion of the freedom to think and speak for oneself.

The Journey to Philadelphia

At the age of 17, young Franklin made a bold decision to leave behind his familiar world and seek adventure in a new city—Philadelphia. With determination in his heart and dreams of a brighter future, he set off on a journey that would shape the course of his life.

Arriving in Philadelphia, Franklin eagerly sought work in various printing shops, hoping to find his place in this bustling city. Yet, none of these opportunities fulfilled his ambitions. However, fate had a remarkable encounter in store for him.

During his early days in Philadelphia, Franklin caught the attention of Pennsylvania's governor, Sir William Keith. Keith saw potential in the young printer and persuaded Franklin to travel to London to acquire the necessary equipment for starting a new newspaper in Philadelphia. Filled with excitement and optimism, Franklin embarked on the journey across the ocean, envisioning a bright future ahead.

Upon reaching London, Franklin soon realized that Governor Keith's promises were empty. Undeterred by this setback, Franklin took up work as a typesetter in a printer's shop located in the historic Church of St Bartholomew-the-Great in the Smithfield area of London. Despite the challenges and disappointments, Franklin's resilience and determination kept him going.

After his stint in London, Franklin returned to Philadelphia in 1726 with the assistance of Thomas Denham, a kind merchant who offered him employment as a clerk, shopkeeper, and bookkeeper in his business. This new opportunity provided Franklin with stability and a chance to develop his skills in commerce and trade further.

Through these experiences, Franklin learned valuable lessons about perseverance, resilience, and the importance of seizing opportunities. His journey to Philadelphia marked the beginning of a transformative chapter in his life—one filled with exploration, setbacks, and, ultimately, triumphs that would pave the way for his remarkable legacy.

A Special Bond

In 1723, when Benjamin Franklin was just 17 years old, he fell in love with a 15-year-old girl named Deborah Read. Benjamin, living as a boarder in the Read household, proposed marriage to Deborah. However, Deborah's mother was cautious about allowing her young daughter to marry Benjamin due to his financial instability and impending journey to London at Governor Keith's request.

While Benjamin was in London, his trip was extended, and Deborah decided to marry another man named John Rodgers. Unfortunately, this marriage turned out to be a mistake. Shortly after their wedding,

Rodgers fled to Barbados with Deborah's dowry, leaving her alone and facing difficult circumstances.

After these challenges, Benjamin and Deborah eventually married on September 1, 1730. They embraced their life together and had two children—Francis Folger Franklin, born in October 1732, and Sarah "Sally" Franklin, born in 1743, who later married Richard Bache.

Deborah never accompanied Benjamin on his extended trips to Europe because of her fear of the sea. This fear, along with Benjamin's frequent travels, meant they spent much time apart. Unfortunately, their son Francis died of smallpox in 1736, causing deep sorrow for the family.

Despite spending a lot of time apart due to Benjamin's frequent travels, Deborah and Benjamin cherished their time together and remained very happy in their relationship. Their love and devotion to each other continued to grow despite the distance between them.

The Birth of the Junto

In the year 1727, a young and ambitious Benjamin Franklin, just 21 years old, embarked on a remarkable journey of intellectual and community enrichment. It was during this time that Franklin formed a group known as the Junto—a gathering of like-minded artisans and tradesmen in Philadelphia who shared a common goal: to better themselves while also improving their community.

The Junto was more than just a social club— it was a place where members engaged in lively discussions on the pressing issues of the day, exchanging ideas and seeking solutions to societal challenges. Inspired by the intellectual fervor of English coffeehouses that Franklin had encountered, the Junto became a hub of Enlightenment ideals, fostering a spirit of curiosity and progress.

Reading played a central role in the Junto's activities. However, books were scarce and expensive in those days. Determined to overcome this obstacle, Franklin proposed a brilliant solution: to create a shared library among the Junto members. He envisioned a place where their collective books could be kept together, allowing each member access to a wide range of knowledge.

Franklin's idea evolved further. Recognizing the need for broader access to books beyond their personal collections, he conceived the notion of a subscription library. This innovative concept involved pooling funds from Junto members to purchase books for the collective benefit of all.

In 1731, Franklin's vision became a reality with the establishment of the Library Company of Philadelphia. This pioneering institution, chartered by Franklin himself, marked the beginning of America's first subscription library. This groundbreaking initiative democratized access to knowledge and paved the way for public libraries across the nation.

Through Franklin's ingenuity and the collaborative efforts of the Junto, the Library Company of Philadelphia flourished, becoming a cornerstone of intellectual life in the burgeoning city. The library's impact extended far beyond its walls, empowering individuals from diverse backgrounds to engage in lifelong learning and contribute to the intellectual growth of their community.

Pages of Influence

After Thomas Denham passed away, Benjamin Franklin returned to his first love—printing. In 1728, when he was just 22 years old, Franklin teamed up with Hugh Meredith to start their own printing business in Philadelphia. The next year, he became the publisher of The Pennsylvania Gazette, a popular newspaper in the city.

Running The Pennsylvania Gazette gave Franklin a chance to share his thoughts on local issues and ideas through essays and observations. People admired Franklin for his sharp mind and hard work, and he gained a lot of respect in Philadelphia. Even as he later became known as a scientist and leader, Franklin stayed down-to-earth, signing his letters simply as "B. Franklin, Printer."

In 1732, Franklin tried something new by publishing America's first German-language newspaper, called Die Philadelphische Zeitung. Although it didn't last long because of competition from other German papers, Franklin's effort showed his desire to reach out to different communities and share knowledge.

Franklin also printed religious books in German for the Moravian community in Bethlehem, Pennsylvania, and became close to them.

But Franklin saw printing as more than just a business. He believed it was a way to teach moral goodness to Americans and serve God.

He used his printing work to try to improve people's behavior.

His impact went beyond Philadelphia. Franklin wanted to connect the colonies, so he helped set up a network of newspapers that reached across colonial America. By 1753, Franklin and his partners were behind eight out of fifteen English-language newspapers in the colonies.

Through his newspapers, Franklin encouraged people to talk about important issues and question authority, which helped create a culture of learning and community involvement. His work as a printer played a big part in shaping American journalism and the independent spirit that led to the Revolutionary War.

The Masonic Path

In the early 1730s, Benjamin Franklin's life in Pennsylvania took an interesting turn when he joined the local Masonic lodge. This was the start of Franklin's lifelong connection with Freemasonry—a group focused on friendship, good morals, and helping each other.

Franklin quickly moved up in the Masonic world and became a grandmaster in 1734, showing how fast he became a leader in Pennsylvania's Masonic group. That same year, he took on a big project by editing and publishing the first Masonic book in America—a new version of James

Anderson's "Constitutions of the Free-Masons."

Franklin didn't just have ceremonial roles in Freemasonry. He was also the secretary of St. John's Lodge in Philadelphia from 1735 to 1738, where he helped run the lodge's activities.

But Franklin faced a tough situation in 1738 when he was involved in a court case about a young apprentice who died during a fake Masonic initiation. Two men were blamed for causing the death during a ritual that went wrong. Franklin knew about what was planned, but he wasn't part of it. Even so, some people criticized him for not doing more to stop it.

Andrew Bradford, who was Franklin's publishing rival, criticized Franklin's role in his newspaper, The American Weekly Mercury. Franklin defended himself in The Pennsylvania Gazette, explaining what happened and why he couldn't prevent the tragedy.

Despite the controversy, Franklin stayed a committed Freemason for the rest of his life. Being part of this group showed Franklin's belief in helping others, being honest, and working together for a better community—a sign of his strong dedication to friendship and good behavior among his friends.

Poor Richard's Pen

In 1732, Benjamin Franklin started something exciting: he began publishing Poor Richard's Almanack under the name Richard Saunders. This special almanac quickly became a favorite, filled with all sorts of useful information.

Even though everyone knew Franklin was behind it, he pretended Richard Saunders was a real person, adding to the fun of the almanac. Poor Richard's Almanack was famous for its simple language, practical tips, and a bit of humor. It was packed with sayings that people loved then and still know today, like "A penny saved is twopence dear" (sometimes said as "A penny saved is a penny earned") and "Fish and visitors stink in three days."

The almanac was a big hit, selling around ten thousand copies every year and becoming super popular in colonial America.

Besides the Almanac, Franklin also tried other publishing projects. In 1741, he started The General Magazine and Historical Chronicle for all the British Plantations in America, which had the Prince of Wales's badge on the cover.

In 1758, Franklin published Father Abraham's Sermon, also known as The Way to Wealth. This booklet provided great advice about being successful and smart with money.

Later in life, Franklin started writing his autobiography in 1771, but it didn't come out until after he passed away. Now, his autobiography is a classic that lots of people read.

Franklin wrote about all sorts of things, from how to behave well to controversial topics. His writing made a big impact on literature and publishing, and people still love and celebrate his work today.

The Spark of Discovery

Benjamin Franklin was always curious about the world around him. In the 1740s, he became really interested in electricity after seeing a lecture by a man named Archibald Spencer. When Spencer demonstrated static electricity, it sparked something in Franklin's mind, and he wanted to learn more about this mysterious force.

Back then, people thought there were two kinds of "electrical fluid": vitreous and resinous. But Franklin had a new idea—he thought these were actually the same electricity, just at different pressures. Another scientist, William Watson, had a similar idea around the same time. Franklin was the first to call these types positive and negative, and he discovered the rule that electricity is always conserved, which means it doesn't disappear—it just moves around.

In 1748, Franklin made something really cool—a multiple-plate capacitor that he called an "electrical battery." This wasn't like the batteries we use today; it was made by stacking eleven glass panes between lead plates, hanging them with silk cords, and connecting them with wires.

Franklin wanted to show that electricity could be useful in everyday life. So, in 1749, he planned a special dinner where he used electricity to cook and roast a turkey. He found out that turkeys cooked by electricity were super tender and delicious!

Once, during an experiment, Franklin accidentally gave himself an electric shock with Leyden jars, a type of capacitor. His arms felt numb for a whole evening afterward, which he called a "big mistake."

Franklin's work with electricity was so amazing that he won a special prize called the Copley Medal from the Royal Society in 1753. He was also chosen to be part of the Society in 1756, which was a big honor for an American back then.

Did you know? The unit of electric charge, called one franklin (Fr), is named after Benjamin Franklin to honor his discoveries in electricity.

Later on, after a fire destroyed Harvard University's first collection of electrical equipment, Franklin helped them get new lab tools. This collection is now part of the Harvard Collection of Historical Scientific Instruments, and you can see it at the Science Center today.

Unraveling the Mysteries of Lightning

Benjamin Franklin was always curious about nature's mysteries, especially electricity. In the 1750s, he wanted to prove that lightning was electricity, but he knew it would be too dangerous to wait for lightning to strike directly. So, he devised a clever experiment using a kite.

On May 10, 1752, in France, someone else successfully tried Franklin's experiment using a tall iron rod to get sparks from a storm cloud. This made Franklin excited to try it himself. Then, on June 15, 1752, in Philadelphia, Franklin may have done a similar experiment. He didn't say he did it in his newspaper, The Pennsylvania Gazette, on October 19, 1752, but he explained how to do it safely.

Instead of waiting for lightning to strike, Franklin used a kite with a key tied to its string. The kite collected electric charge from a storm cloud, showing that lightning was electricity. Franklin explained how to do the experiment safely in a letter to England, proving that the electrical matter in lightning was the same as in other electrical experiments.

Franklin's experiments with electricity led to an important invention—the lightning rod. He figured out that a conductor with a sharp point could discharge lightning quietly and from farther away. To protect buildings from lightning strikes, Franklin suggested putting sharp iron rods attached to wires that ran into the ground. This way, the lightning's electrical fire would go away from the building before it could cause harm.

After successful tests on his own house, people started putting lightning rods on important buildings like the Academy of Philadelphia and the Pennsylvania State House (later known as Independence Hall) in 1752. Thanks to Benjamin Franklin's discoveries, we now have safer ways to protect buildings from the dangers of lightning strikes.

Exploring Light, Storms, and Cool Breezes

Benjamin Franklin loved exploring the mysteries of nature all around him. He was interested in how light worked and supported Christiaan Huygens's idea that light moves in waves, even though most people believed Isaac Newton's idea that light was made of tiny particles. It took until Thomas Young's experiments in 1803 for scientists to really agree with Huygens.

In 1743, during a storm, Franklin noticed something unusual. He saw that the wind was blowing in a different direction from where the storm was moving. This discovery challenged what people thought about weather and helped scientists understand more about how storms work.

When Europe had a harsh winter in 1784 because of a big volcanic eruption in Iceland, Franklin started to study how different events in nature are connected. This was one of the first times someone looked into how nature affects our environment.

Besides his famous experiments with lightning and kites, Franklin also used kites to pull people and even boats across water, which inspired others to use kites for power like George Pocock.

Franklin was also curious about cooling by evaporation. On a hot day, he found that wearing a wet shirt in the wind kept him cooler than a dry one. In 1758, he and another scientist, John Hadley, used evaporating liquid to cool down a thermometer, showing how refrigeration works.

He also studied how different colors absorb heat. Franklin noticed that dark-colored clothes soak up more heat than lighter ones. He tested this by putting different-colored pieces of cloth in the snow on a sunny day and saw that black cloth got the hottest.

Franklin even investigated how well things conduct electricity. He found that ice doesn't conduct electricity like water does. He also discovered that putting a little bit of oil on rough water can instantly calm it, which is why he carried oil in his walking stick to calm choppy waters.

Exploring Population Growth

Benjamin Franklin wasn't just curious about electricity and politics—he also found the study of population growth, called demography, fascinating. In the 1730s and 1740s, he started taking careful notes on how populations changed over time. What he discovered amazed him—America had the fastest-growing population in the world!

Franklin thought that population growth depended on having enough food to eat and lots of land to farm. He figured out that America's population was doubling every 20 years and predicted that it would eventually be even bigger than England's population within a hundred years.

In 1751, Franklin wrote a famous document called "Observations concerning the Increase of Mankind, Peopling of Countries, etc." This document talked about how populations grow and what makes them grow. Four years later, it was printed anonymously in Boston and became popular in Britain. Even economists like Adam Smith read it, and later, demographers like Thomas Malthus credited Franklin with discovering important rules about population growth.

Franklin's predictions worried British leaders, who didn't like the idea of the American colonies becoming more powerful. They started putting more restrictions on trade to try to keep control.

Franklin's writings about population growth are still important today. They're some of the most famous works about demography from the 1700s, showing that people back then really paid attention to what he had to say. Franklin also studied how slavery affected populations, looking at how it changed things.

Besides studying population, Franklin wrote about money issues, such as controlling prices, trade rules, and helping poor people. His ideas were important and are still studied today by people interested in how populations grow and how money works.

MARK LYLANI

A Path to Public Service

In 1736, Benjamin Franklin showed his inventiveness by starting the Union Fire Company, one of America's first groups of volunteer firefighters. At the same time, he found clever ways to stop people from making fake money by printing new currency for New Jersey.

Franklin believed in using paper money to help keep economies stable. In a famous booklet called A Modest Enquiry into the Nature and Necessity of a Paper Currency, which he wrote in 1729, he explained how using paper money could help places that didn't have enough money without raising prices too much.

As Franklin got older, he became more involved in helping his community. In 1743, he had a big idea to start a school in Philadelphia where kids could learn important things. Even though it was tough at first, Franklin's hard work paid off when the school opened in 1751, which later became the University of Pennsylvania.

In 1743, Franklin also started the American Philosophical Society, where smart people could talk about new discoveries and ideas. He was always busy with science, especially his experiments with electricity, which fascinated him just as much as his work in politics.

During King George's War, when Philadelphia's leaders were slow to protect the city, Franklin took matters into his own hands. He raised money to build defenses like walls and cannons, forming what was called the "Association Battery."

By 1747, Franklin had made enough money from his printing business to retire and try other kinds of work. He teamed up with David Hall, and their business did very well, giving Franklin more time for studying and scientific experiments.

Franklin also cared about people's health and safety. In 1751, he helped start the Pennsylvania Hospital to treat sick people. He also set up the Philadelphia Contributionship, which was the first company to offer insurance for people's homes in the colonies.

During the 1750s, Franklin and his friends changed how colleges worked. They believed in teaching in English and focusing on practical skills without asking people about their religion to get in. Their ideas helped shape many colleges in America.

In 1754, Franklin led a group from Pennsylvania to a meeting called the Albany Congress. He had a plan to join all the colonies together to defend against enemies, but not everyone agreed with him. Even so, Franklin's ideas planted seeds for future ideas that would shape the United States.

Architect of America's Mail Network"

In 1737, Benjamin Franklin was given a special job in Philadelphia—he became the postmaster. That meant he was in charge of making sure letters and packages were sent to the right places. He kept this job until 1753 when he was appointed as the deputy postmaster-general of all the British colonies in North America. This was a big deal because it was the first time someone shared this important role with another person, William Hunter.

Benjamin Franklin's job covered a huge area—from Pennsylvania to Newfoundland.

He worked hard to improve the postal service, making it faster to deliver mail between cities like Philadelphia, New York, and Boston. Because of his improvements, the colonial post office started making money by 1761.

When the British took over new lands in 1763 and created Quebec, Franklin saw a chance to expand mail services to cities like Montreal, Quebec City, and New York.

For many years, Franklin lived in England to do his postal work, but he always remembered where he came from—America. When the American Revolution began, Franklin's support for independence got him kicked out of his job in 1774.

After America declared independence in 1776, it needed its own postal system. The leaders of the new country chose Benjamin Franklin as the first postmaster general of the United States Post Office.

His apprentice, William Goddard, believed that his ideas played a significant role in shaping the postal system, and he thought he should have been chosen for the post. However, he graciously accepted Benjamin Franklin's appointment. Franklin recognized Goddard's talents and appointed him Surveyor of the Posts. He gave Goddard a signed pass and entrusted him with investigating and inspecting post offices and mail routes as needed.

The postal system that Benjamin Franklin helped set up back then is the same one we use today in the United States!

Discovering the Gulf Stream

While working as deputy postmaster, Benjamin Franklin's curiosity led him to explore the mysteries of the ocean, especially the North Atlantic Ocean's currents. In 1768, when he was in England, Franklin heard about an interesting problem from the Colonial Board of Customs. They noticed that British mail ships, called packet ships, took much longer to reach New York compared to merchant ships sailing to Newport, Rhode Island. This got Franklin curious, and he wanted to figure out why.

Franklin asked his cousin, Timothy Folger, who was an experienced whaler captain from Nantucket, for help. Captain Folger explained that merchant ships had a smart way of sailing to avoid a strong eastbound ocean current that slowed down the mail packet ships. The packet captains sailed directly into this tough current, which made them go slower by 3 miles per hour (5 km/h). This idea fascinated Franklin, and he worked together with Folger and other ship captains to study and map this ocean current.

Franklin's hard work led to an amazing discovery—he mapped and named the ocean current the "Gulf Stream." In 1770, Franklin published his Gulf Stream map in England, but not many people noticed it. However, later versions printed in France in 1778 and the United States in 1786 got more attention.

It's interesting to note that the original British edition of Franklin's map was thought to be lost forever until a Woods

Hole oceanographer named Phil Richardson found it in the Bibliothèque Nationale in Paris in 1980, and this discovery made news in The New York Times.

It took some time for British sea captains to accept Franklin's discoveries and change their sailing routes accordingly. But once they did, they were able to shorten their sailing time by about two weeks.

Even though Franklin didn't technically "discover" the Gulf Stream (since earlier explorers already knew about it), he played a really important role in mapping and explaining its path so that sailors could use it better. Franklin's ocean findings were written down in a book called "Maritime Observations," which was published by the Philosophical Society's transactions in 1786. This book had cool ideas for sea anchors, shipboard lightning rods, and even a special soup bowl that wouldn't spill during stormy seas—a great example of Franklin's creative mind and love for exploring new things.

Standing Up to Power

In 1757, Benjamin Franklin traveled from Pennsylvania to England to speak up against the powerful Penn family, who had a lot of control in the colony. The Penn family could change laws made by the elected Assembly and didn't have to pay taxes like everyone else, which Franklin thought was unfair.

He stayed in England for five years, trying to convince the government to stop the Penn family from changing laws and avoiding taxes. But Franklin didn't have enough powerful friends in London to make it happen, and his mission didn't succeed.

When Franklin came back to Pennsylvania, he led a group called the "anti-proprietary party." They wanted to reduce the Penn family's control because people were unhappy about it. In 1764, Franklin was elected Speaker of the Pennsylvania House, but he made a mistake by suggesting changing the government to be ruled by the king. People in Pennsylvania were worried about losing their freedoms, so Franklin lost his seat in the Assembly in 1764 because of these fears and attacks on his character.

The anti-proprietary party sent Franklin back to England to keep fighting against the Penn family's rule. While he was in London, Franklin strongly opposed a law called the Stamp Act in 1765, even though he couldn't stop it from passing. But then he made another mistake by recommending a friend for a job distributing stamps in Pennsylvania, which made people think he supported the Stamp Act. Pennsylvanians were so angry that they threatened to destroy Franklin's house in Philadelphia.

However, Franklin soon realized how much the American colonies were against the Stamp Act. He spoke in front of the House of Commons and helped get the Stamp Act canceled. Suddenly, Franklin became the top spokesperson for American interests in England. He wrote many essays supporting the colonies, and Georgia, New Jersey, and Massachusetts all asked him to represent them to the British king.

While in London, Franklin stayed at a house on Craven Street. He became friends with his landlady, Margaret Stevenson, and her daughter Mary, also known as Polly. This house is now the Benjamin Franklin House museum. In London, Franklin also joined a group called "the honest Whigs," which met with other important people who wanted to make changes.

Defending Against Danger

In 1763, when Benjamin Franklin came back to Pennsylvania from England, the western frontier was in trouble because of Pontiac's Rebellion. During this difficult time, a group of settlers called the Paxton Boys became convinced that the Pennsylvania government wasn't doing enough to protect them from American Indian attacks. They were scared and angry, so they did something terrible—they attacked and killed peaceful Susquehannock Indians.

The situation got worse as the Paxton Boys marched toward Philadelphia, threatening the capital with their armed group. Benjamin

Franklin knew he had to act fast. He gathered support and organized a local militia to defend Philadelphia against the approaching mob.

Franklin was known for his ability to talk and persuade people. He met with the Paxton leaders to try to make peace and stop more violence. By talking calmly and appealing to their sense of fairness and kindness, Franklin convinced the Paxton Boys to go back home and end the threat.

After the violence, Franklin wrote a strong criticism, condemning what the Paxton Boys had done and challenging their unfair beliefs. He believed that one person's actions shouldn't lead to blame on a whole group of people.

During this tough time, Franklin also used clever methods to protect American interests from British spying. He worked on public relations, asked for secret help, and even supported private expeditions to fight against enemy ships.

Journeys Across Europe and Beyond

In London, Benjamin Franklin used the city as a starting point for his adventures. In 1771, he went on short journeys around England, staying with friends like Joseph Priestley in Leeds, Thomas Percival in Manchester, and Erasmus Darwin in Lichfield. He even spent time in Scotland, visiting Lord Kames near Stirling and staying for weeks with David Hume in Edinburgh. Franklin loved his time in Scotland, calling it "six weeks of the happiest time I have experienced in any part of my life."

During a visit to Ireland, Franklin stayed with Lord Hillsborough, who seemed nice at first but turned out to be quite demanding. In Dublin, Franklin received a special honor—he was allowed to sit with the members of the Irish Parliament instead of sitting in the gallery like other visitors. This made him the first American to receive such an honor. As he traveled around Ireland, Franklin was deeply affected by the poverty he saw, realizing that Ireland faced similar challenges to those of the American colonies due to trade regulations and laws.

Franklin also traveled to German lands for two months in 1766, and his connection to Germany lasted his whole life. He was grateful to German scientist Otto von Guericke for his early studies on electricity. In 1785, Franklin co-authored the first treaty of friendship between Prussia and America.

Later, in September 1767, Franklin visited Paris with his friend Sir John Pringle. In France, news of Franklin's discoveries about electricity had already spread, and his reputation helped him meet important scientists, politicians, and even King Louis XV.

Maestro of Music and Chess

Benjamin Franklin was not only a brilliant scientist and inventor but also a talented musician and chess enthusiast.

During his time in London, Franklin developed an improved version of the glass harmonica, a musical instrument made of spinning glass bowls that produced hauntingly beautiful sounds when played. His innovative design involved rotating the glasses on a shaft while keeping the player's fingers steady. This new version quickly gained popularity across Europe, with renowned composers like Mozart and Beethoven composing music specifically for Franklin's glass harmonica.

Aside from the glass harmonica, Franklin played several musical instruments, including the violin, harp, and guitar. He even composed a string quartet in the early classical style, showcasing his musical talent and creativity.

In addition to his musical pursuits, Franklin was an avid chess player. He started playing chess around 1733, making him the first known chess player in the American colonies. Franklin loved chess so much that he wrote an essay titled "The Morals of Chess," where he praised the game's virtues and outlined a code of conduct for players. This essay became widely popular and has been translated into many languages.

Franklin used chess as a tool for learning, even using it to practice Italian with a friend. The winner of their chess games would assign tasks related to learning Italian to the loser before their next match.

During his time in England and France, Franklin frequented coffee houses known for chess, where he played against skilled opponents and honed his chess skills. His passion for the game earned him a spot in the U.S. Chess Hall of Fame, and a chess club in Philadelphia, the Franklin Mercantile Chess Club, was named in his honor.

Standing Up for America

In Parliament, there was an argument about whether Americans should help pay for the costs of the French and Indian War. They wanted to impose new taxes on the colonies. In 1766, Franklin was chosen to speak for the Americans in front of Parliament. He explained that Americans had already done a lot to defend the British Empire. Local governments had raised money, sent soldiers, and spent millions to fight France during the war.

In 1772, Franklin got hold of private letters from Thomas Hutchinson and Andrew Oliver, who were in charge in Massachusetts. These letters showed they wanted the British government to be tough on Bostonians. Franklin sent these letters to America, and when they were made public in a newspaper, it caused a big uproar. The British were not happy with Franklin and thought he was causing trouble.

Things got worse in 1774 when Franklin was treated badly by the British government during a hearing. He decided to return to Philadelphia in 1775 and changed his stance on how to deal with the British.

In 1773, Franklin wrote two famous essays that made fun of British policies towards America: "Rules by Which a Great Empire May Be Reduced to a Small One" and "An Edict by the King of Prussia."

A New Chapter Begins

When Benjamin Franklin came back to Philadelphia on May 5, 1775, after his second trip to Great Britain, he found his homeland caught up in the early moments of the American Revolution. Just a month earlier, in April 1775, the Battles of Lexington and Concord had started the fight, marking the beginning of this important struggle for independence. Patriots across the colonies were taking up arms against British rule, and in New England, militia forces had managed to contain the main British army in Boston.

When Franklin returned, his respected reputation and leadership skills led the Pennsylvania Assembly to choose him as their delegate to the Second Continental Congress. This congress, which brought together representatives from all the colonies, was meeting to coordinate the colonies' response to British actions and guide the revolution.

In June 1776, Franklin was chosen for a special committee to write a document declaring America's determination for independence—the Declaration of Independence. Even though he was struggling with gout and couldn't attend many meetings, Franklin shared his smart ideas during the drafting process. He carefully looked over the draft made by Thomas Jefferson and suggested some "small but important" changes that made the document clearer and stronger.

When it came time to sign the Declaration of Independence, Franklin's famous wit and practical thinking came out. John Hancock said they all had to "hang together," meaning they needed to stay united. Franklin joked back, saying, "Yes, we must, indeed, all hang together, or most assuredly, we shall all hang separately."

Franklin knew they were facing big risks and understood how important it was to stick together in their fight for freedom from British rule. By saying they had to "hang together," Franklin meant they had to stand united and support each other. He knew that if they didn't work together, they might face serious consequences on their own. Essentially, Franklin reminded them that their future was connected to their teamwork and to backing each other up.

Benjamin Franklin's return to Philadelphia was the start of a new chapter in his amazing life—a chapter defined by his strong commitment to America's journey for independence and his big role in shaping history.

Diplomacy and Discoveries

During the American Revolution, Benjamin Franklin was sent to France in 1776 as a commissioner for the United States. He brought his 16-year-old grandson, William Temple Franklin, along as his secretary. They settled in Passy, a suburb of Paris, in a home donated by Jacques-Donatien Le Ray de Chaumont, a supporter of the United States.

Franklin stayed in France until 1785 and handled America's affairs with the French nation successfully. One of his major accomplishments was securing a critical military alliance between France and the

United States in 1778. This alliance greatly aided the American cause against Britain.

While in France, Franklin also played a key role in negotiating and signing the Treaty of Paris in 1783, which officially ended the American Revolutionary War.

In addition to his diplomatic duties, Franklin had influential associates in France, including Honoré Gabriel Riqueti, comte de Mirabeau, who was a prominent French writer, orator, and statesman during the French Revolution. Franklin contributed anonymously to Mirabeau's work, which criticized the Society of the Cincinnati—a prestigious order established in the United States—because it conflicted with the egalitarian ideals of the new republic.

Franklin was also active as a Freemason in France, serving as venerable master of the lodge Les Neuf Sœurs from 1779 to 1781.

In 1784, Franklin was part of a commission appointed by Louis XVI to investigate the theory of "animal magnetism" proposed by Franz Mesmer. The commission's findings discredited mesmerism, attributing its effects to the power of suggestion rather than any supernatural force.

Franklin's advocacy for religious tolerance in France contributed to Louis XVI's signing of the Edict of Versailles in 1787, which nullified previous laws restricting the rights of non-Catholics.

During his time in France, Franklin also served as the American minister to Sweden and negotiated a treaty that was signed in April 1783.

Franklin's enthusiasm for science was evident when he witnessed the world's first hydrogen balloon flight in Paris on August 27, 1783. He financially supported subsequent balloon projects and was an honored guest at the Jardin des Tuileries for another notable flight in December 1783.

Benjamin Franklin's contributions and diplomatic efforts in France were instrumental in securing vital support for the American Revolution and fostering important international relations that helped shape the new United States.

Champion of Independence and Abolition

When Benjamin Franklin returned home to America in 1785 after his successful diplomatic mission in France, he was hailed as one of the most important figures in the fight for American independence, second only to George Washington. However, there was some controversy surrounding his return.

During his time in France, there was an unexplained shortage of 100,000 pounds in Congressional funds. When a member of congress asked Franklin about this missing money, Franklin cleverly responded by quoting a passage from the Bible, saying, "Muzzle not the ox that treadeth out his master's grain." This wise saying suggested that those who work hard should be allowed to enjoy the fruits of their labor. The missing funds were never brought up again in congress.

Despite this controversy, Jacques-Donatien Le Ray de Chaumont honored Franklin with a commissioned portrait painted by Joseph Duplessis. This famous portrait now hangs in the National Portrait Gallery of the Smithsonian Institution in Washington, D.C.

After returning to America, Franklin's views on slavery underwent a significant change. He became an abolitionist and decided to free his two slaves. Franklin's dedication to ending slavery continued, and he eventually became the president of the Pennsylvania

Abolition Society, working tirelessly to bring an end to this unjust practice.

MARK LYLANI

96

Leading Pennsylvania

In October 1785, Benjamin Franklin was chosen by unanimous vote to become the sixth president of the Supreme Executive Council of Pennsylvania. This role was similar to that of a governor. This honor was bestowed upon him after he succeeded John Dickinson in this important office. Franklin's election was a testament to his respected status and the trust he earned among the people of Pennsylvania.

During his tenure as president, Franklin held the office for just over three years, making him the longest-serving president of the council. He adhered to the constitutional limit of three full terms in office, which reflected his commitment to upholding democratic principles.

Soon after his initial election, Franklin was re-elected for a full term on October 29, 1785, and subsequently in the fall of 1786 and on October 31, 1787. Throughout this period, he played a pivotal role in the governance of Pennsylvania.

One of Franklin's most significant contributions during his presidency was hosting the Constitutional Convention of 1787 in Philadelphia. This historic event brought together delegates from various states to deliberate and draft a new constitution for the United States. Franklin's presence at the convention was influential, even though he primarily served as a symbolic figure and rarely engaged in debates.

Despite his esteemed position as president of Pennsylvania, it's important to note that Benjamin Franklin never served as the president of the United States. However, his impact on American history and governance remains profound, particularly through his contributions to the drafting of the U.S. Constitution and his unwavering dedication to the ideals of democracy and liberty.

A Life Remembered

Benjamin Franklin faced health challenges, especially in his later years. His struggles with obesity led to various health issues, including severe gout. As he aged, these health problems worsened. During the signing of the U.S. Constitution in 1787, Franklin's health was poor, and afterward, he withdrew from public life.

Sadly, Franklin passed away from a pleuritic attack on April 17, 1790, at his home in Philadelphia. He was 84 years old at the time of his death. His final words, reportedly spoken to his daughter, were, "a dying man can do nothing easy." His health deteriorated further when an abscess in his lungs burst, making it hard for him to breathe. Eventually, he peacefully passed away around eleven o'clock at night.

Around 20,000 people attended Franklin's funeral, a testament to the deep respect and admiration people had for him. He was laid to rest in Christ Church Burial Ground in Philadelphia. When news of his death reached Revolutionary France, the Constitutional Assembly entered a period of mourning, and memorial services were held across the country to honor Franklin's legacy.

In 1728, at just 22 years old, Franklin penned what he hoped would be his epitaph:

"The Body of B. Franklin Printer; Like the Cover of an old Book, Its Contents torn out, And stript of its Lettering and Gilding, Lies here, Food for Worms. But the work shall not be wholly lost: For it will, as he believ'd, appear once more, In a new & more perfect Edition, Corrected and Amended By the Author."

However, Franklin's actual grave, as specified in his final will, simply reads "Benjamin and Deborah Franklin." This reflects his modesty and the love he shared with his wife, Deborah.

Honors and Innovations

In 1756, Benjamin Franklin joined the Society for the Encouragement of Arts, Manufactures & Commerce, which later became known as the Royal Society of Arts. This society supported and promoted new ideas in science, art, and business. When Franklin returned to the United States in 1775, he kept in touch with this group and became a Corresponding Member.

The Royal Society of Arts honored Franklin by creating the Benjamin Franklin Medal in 1956, which celebrated the 250th anniversary of his birth and the 200th anniversary of his membership in the society.

Franklin loved learning about science and was friends with many other scientists. He was part of a special group called the Lunar Society of Birmingham, which was filled with brilliant thinkers. In 1759, the University of St Andrews in Scotland gave Franklin an honorary doctorate to recognize all his amazing accomplishments. They even made him a "Freeman" of their city.

Oxford University also awarded Franklin an honorary doctorate in 1762. Because of these awards, people started calling him "Dr. Franklin."

While living in London in 1768, Franklin devised a new way of writing that he thought would simplify spelling. He created a different alphabet and spelling system that eliminated some unnecessary letters and added new ones for sounds that didn't have their own letters. However, not many people used this new system, and Franklin eventually lost interest in it.

A Legacy of Innovation and Influence

In recognition of Benjamin Franklin's diverse contributions, a Pennsylvania Historical Marker stands proudly in Philadelphia, marking the place where he lived during the final years of his life. Erected on June 30, 1990, the marker honors Franklin's achievements as a printer, author, inventor, diplomat, philanthropist, statesman, and scientist.

Benjamin Franklin's enduring generosity extended beyond his lifetime through a thoughtful bequest to the cities of Boston and Philadelphia. In his will, Franklin left

£1,000 for each city to be held in trust for 200 years, with the aim of gathering interest to benefit future generations. The funds accumulated substantially over the years, with Philadelphia amassing more than $2 million by 1990 and Boston nearly $5 million.

Franklin's influence is felt through his deeds and ubiquitous image. As one of the only signatories of the Declaration of Independence, the Treaty of Alliance with France, the Treaty of Paris, and the U.S. Constitution, Franklin holds a unique place in American history. He is often humorously referred to as "the only president of the United States who was never president of the United States."

Franklin's likeness graces various forms of currency, including the $100 bill since 1914. He also appeared on the half-dollar from

1948 to 1963 and on other denominations, such as the $50 bill and several iterations of the $100 bill from 1914 and 1918. Additionally, Franklin's image has been featured on U.S. postage stamps numerous times, more frequently than almost any other notable American, except George Washington.

In 1976, during America's bicentennial celebration, congress dedicated a towering marble statue at Philadelphia's Franklin Institute—the Benjamin Franklin National Memorial. Today, many of Franklin's personal possessions are on display at the institute, preserving his legacy for future generations.

Benjamin Franklin's former residence at 36 Craven Street in London has been transformed into the Benjamin Franklin House, open to the public and marked with a blue plaque. This house reveals intriguing historical insights, including the discovery of buried remains believed to be associated with anatomical studies conducted by William Hewson during Franklin's time there.

CONCLUSION

As we come to the end of our exploration of Benjamin Franklin's life and legacy, we find ourselves inspired by his incredible achievements. From his early days as a printer's apprentice to his role as a Founding Father of the United States, Franklin's journey is a testament to the power of curiosity, ingenuity, and perseverance.

Throughout this book, we've journeyed alongside Franklin as he unraveled the mysteries of electricity, championed the cause of American independence, and pioneered innovations that continue to impact our lives today. We've marveled at his experiments, celebrated his inventions, and admired his unwavering commitment to knowledge and progress.

Benjamin Franklin's story teaches us valuable lessons: the importance of lifelong learning, the impact of innovation on society, and the value of daring to question the status quo. His boundless curiosity and relentless pursuit of improvement serve as an inspiration to curious minds everywhere.

As we reflect on Franklin's life, let us remember that each of us has the potential to make a difference. Whether through scientific exploration, creative invention, or civic engagement, we can follow in Franklin's footsteps by embracing curiosity, embracing challenges, and striving to leave a positive impact on the world around us.

So, as we close this chapter on Benjamin Franklin, let us carry forward the spirit of inquiry and innovation that defined his life. Let us continue to ask questions, seek answers, and forge our own paths of discovery. And may Benjamin Franklin's legacy serve as a guiding light for generations of curious minds yet to come.

Thank you for joining us on this journey through history. Remember, the adventure of knowledge never ends—it only awaits the next curious soul to embark upon it.

Made in United States
North Haven, CT
18 November 2024